IMAGES
of Modern America

LGBT BALTIMORE

On the Front Cover: Clockwise from top left:
Baltimore Justice Campaign members Mayor Kurt Schmoke and council president Mary Pat Clarke at the signing of the lesbian and gay rights bill in June 1988 (Courtesy the Gay, Lesbian, Bisexual, and Transgender Community Center of Baltimore and Central Maryland Archives at the University of Baltimore [GLCCB Archives]), Men of the Rainbow entertain Baltimore Pride Day 1998 in Druid Hill Park (Courtesy GLCCB Archives), GLCCB banner at 2000 Pride Parade (Courtesy GLCCB Archives), Metropolitan Community Church Baltimore, Baltimore's oldest LGBT organization, in the 1986 Pride Parade (Courtesy Rev. Delores Berry), Blacks United for Gay and Lesbian Equality (BUGLE) struts in the parade on Maryland Avenue in June 1990, with Louis Hughes, founder, third from the right (Courtesy Louis Hughes Jr.)

On the Back Cover: From left to right:
The Chase Brexton Clinic, an AIDS service provider founded by gay men, in the 1993 Pride Parade (Courtesy GLCCB Archives), a proud gay dad with his children in Baltimore in 2005 (Courtesy GLCCB Archives), the Baltimore Justice Campaign team in the Pride Parade in June 1988 (Courtesy Mardie Walker)

IMAGES
of Modern America

LGBT Baltimore

Louise Parker Kelley

ARCADIA
PUBLISHING

Published by Arcadia Publishing
Charleston, South Carolina

Printed in the United States of America

Library of Congress Control Number: 2015931185

For all general information, please contact Arcadia Publishing:
Telephone 843-853-2070
Fax 843-853-0044
E-mail sales@arcadiapublishing.com
For customer service and orders:
Toll-Free 1-888-313-2665

Visit us on the Internet at www.arcadiapublishing.com

This book is dedicated to all those warriors of the heart and everyone who took the risk of coming out and then kept coming out everywhere he or she went, particularly those who said to others, "You can come out in Baltimore, hon, I've got your back."

CONTENTS

Acknowledgments   6

Introduction   7

1.   When LGBT Liberation Was New   11

2.   Out and Never Going Back   31

3.   From Strength to Strength   59

4.   Gaily Forward   77

ACKNOWLEDGMENTS

Thanks go to Caitrin Cunningham, Gillian Nicol, Kris McDonagh, and all those who toiled away at Arcadia Publishing in South Carolina getting this book published. Thanks go to all GLCCB volunteers past and present, particularly those who worked on the Archives Committee, on Pride Day, and on the *Baltimore Gay Paper*, and to *Gay Life* editor Dan McEvily. Thanks go to assistant editors Richard Oloizia, a retired reference librarian for Enoch Pratt Free Library, and Ben Blake, a university archivist at the University of Baltimore, Langsdale Library. Thanks go to University of Baltimore Langsdale Library director Lucy Holman for her enthusiastic support for the project; Thomas Hollowak, retired Langsdale Library head of special collections, for initiating the university's participation in the GLCCB archives project; Laura Melamed, Langsdale Library service assistant, for helping create the image inventory; and the Langsdale Library Special Collections team for their additional support. Thanks also go to Shirley Parry, Mardie Walker, Janet Goldstein, Theresa Palomar, Steve Charing, Greg Satorie, Jeff MacCrae, Claudia Leight, Mike Chase, Barry Kessler, Jim White, Rik and Paulie Newton Treadway, Joel Tinsley Hall, Joanne Riley, Dr. Roger Enlow, Lynda Dee, Shawna Alexander, Beulah Lamont, Gail Vivino, Dana Beyer, John Hannay, John Palen, Maggie McIntosh, Mary Washington, Ann Gordon, Kelly Neel, David Carroll, Cheryl Parham, Donna M. Cartwright, Ruth, Toby, Patti, Allison, Annette Kalandros, John Waters, Pat Moran, Parren Mitchell, Mayor Stephanie Rawlings Blake (the first person to marry gay couples in Maryland), Barbara Mikulski, Kurt Schmoke, Martin O'Malley, Mary Pat Clarke, Scott Stamford, Joyce Kramer, Tammy Carnes Ball, Goldie Mason, Elliot Brager, Bill Urban, Dr. Gillian van Blerk, Sue Sowbel, the New Wave Singers, the Baltimore Men's Chorus, Dignity Baltimore, Theatre Closet, Venus Rising Women's Theater, MCC Baltimore, the 31st Bookstore founders and the Bookstore Cooperative, Black and White Men Together, Brother Help Thyself, Shipmates, Lambda Rising Baltimore (especially Jack Garman), the Waxter Center, the Baltimore Heritage Foundation, the Enoch Pratt Library, the University of Baltimore Special Collections, Johns Hopkins, Morgan State University, Towson University, the *Baltimore Sun*, Atomic Books, Red Emma's, the Drinkery, the Muses, the Women's Growth Center, Ann Singleton, Twila MacDonough, Patrick Alexander, Arnie VandeBrake, Carrie Evans, the Chase Brexton Clinic staff and volunteers past and present, and to Baltimore's many friendly and helpful bartenders.

The source of each photograph is given in a courtesy line accompanying the photograph. If no courtesy line is given, the photograph came from the archives of the Gay, Lesbian, Bisexual, and Transgender Community Center of Baltimore and Central Maryland, housed at the Langsdale Library of the University of Baltimore.

Thanks go to all those charming bisexual leaders, proud drag queens, openly gay men, wise old activists, and fierce lesbian feminists who collected snapshots from everywhere and donated them for use in this book or to the LGBT Archives at UB. Thanks to you, we are invisible no more.

INTRODUCTION

In less than 50 years, lesbian, gay, bisexual and transgendered people have changed the sanctimonious, homophobic culture that once flowed through the city of Baltimore. Dismissed and despised in the 1950s, LGBT people were a significant part of the counterculture of the 1960s. We decided we were going to demand the rights of full citizenship. We did it with persistence, using practical strategies and camp humor. We learned from the radical civil rights movement, the peace movement, and women's liberation to break free and re-create Maryland's largest city in ways that worked.

LGBT people are, and will always be, different. Some places had a grudging acceptance, such as the theater, art museums, certain colleges; drag performers appeared in a few discreet clubs (never gay-owned, however). The Pansy Ball was an annual drag event at the "colored" Elks Club during the Great Depression, as covered by the *Afro American* in March 1932. We worked in every profession—nurses, teachers, city planners, and waiters. But Baltimore was never a safe haven for homosexuals. There were bar raids, such as the one at the Pepper Mill in October 1955 that saw 162 people arrested, which resulted in Judge Cullen scolding the police and dismissing the charges. Epithets such as "queer," "bull dagger," "faggot," "pervert," and "dyke" were commonplace, and the insults often escalated to beatings, arrests, and a high rate of suicide. Gay was not good. It was dangerous, particularly if you could not pass for straight. LGBT citizens were deemed criminals, mentally ill, traitors, worthless, weird, weak, and that huge calumny—child-molesting monsters.

Years after young Johns Hopkins medical student Gertrude Stein had her first love affair with a woman in Baltimore, after bisexual Billie Holiday died young of an overdose, after poet Frank O'Hara died on Fire Island, after various local politicians concealed their preference for the love that at that point did not dare speak its name, a change began with a simple step—coming out. Closets were stuffy and deadly. It was hard to fit a lover in one as well; many relationships did not last. It was time to switch LGBT from being a toxic secret or a sinful tragedy to a source of strength and pride. Coming out became a powerful antidote to life in the closet.

In New York, drag queens, hustlers, and dykes had a riot in June 1969 when the police raided the Stonewall Inn in Greenwich Village, and the revolution moved past discussions in parlors to the real world.

Baltimore was gradually influenced by the sea changes coming from New York and San Francisco, but the process was hardly the same in this blue-collar (Bethlehem Steel, McCormick Spice), heavily Catholic port city.

John Waters filmed *Eat Your Makeup* here in 1968 and *Mondo Trasho*, starring Divine, in 1969. Metropolitan Community Church (MCC), a national church founded and run by LGBT Christians, began in 1972 in Baltimore, and featured integrated leadership from its inception; Rev. Stan Harris, the white gay male pastor, was assisted by an African American woman, Rev. Lapaula Turner. MCC provided space for the gay STD clinic (later part of the Gay Community Center of Baltimore, now the independent Chase Brexton Health Services).

Women, a Journal of Liberation, began publication in 1969, and *Desperate Living*, a national lesbian newsletter based in Baltimore, was first published in 1973. The Gay Liberation Front formed as a collective but disappeared quickly in 1969. The lesbian feminist Ida Brayman Collective on Homestead Street in Waverly, which began in 1972, lasted much longer, and some collective alumni (Jennie Boyd Bull, Ann Gordon) later became leaders in the effort to get equal rights protection for LGBT citizens. The 31st Street Bookstore was a feminist business that flourished with strong support from the nascent lesbian community; it opened in 1973. Business partners Francine Brown and Betsy Bean Millman sold books and magazines for women and children. The bookstore was a vital community resource until it closed in 1995.

The Hippo, a gay-owned bar and dance club, opened in 1972 and is still popular today. Owner Charles Bowers made generous contributions to many Pride Day celebrations. Club Mitchell, a lesbian club owned by a lesbian and transgendered man, began on Pratt Street in 1977. The oldest continuously operating gay bar is Leon's in Mount Vernon. This bar was a speakeasy during the Prohibition era; it has been a gay bar since 1957. Clubs for black gays and lesbians included the Children's Place on Howard Street, Club Bunns, Tikki's, and Paradise Inn, also known as Jones'. Bars for LGBT clientele opened in Waverly, Fells Point, East and South Baltimore; some lasted, many did not; some closed within three months. The Lesbian Community Center, which was established in 1974 and survived until the early 1980s, included an information switchboard, as well as social and cultural events in a shared space with the Women's Liberation Center on Twenty-fifth Street, and later on Greenmount Avenue in the People's Free Medical Clinic.

In 1975, the first Pride rally was held at the Washington Monument in Mount Vernon. The Baltimore Gay Alliance also began in 1975, holding meetings in a member's apartment in Mount Vernon. BGA was committed to creating gay liberation in Baltimore. It published a newsletter via a donated mimeograph machine, began a switchboard, and held a variety of events. The group concluded that it needed 501(c)3 status—to become a nonprofit charity— in order to get health department funding for the then independent men's STD clinic.

In the spring of 1977, the community activists of BGA founded the Gay Community Center of Baltimore (GCCB). The GCCB, which later changed its name to the Gay, Lesbian, Bisexual, and Transgender Community Center of Baltimore and Central Maryland, elected a black woman as president, and immediately began providing services. More space was soon needed, and the center rented basement office space at 2133 Maryland Avenue in 1978. The STD clinic used one side, and the center used the other. In 1978, the Baltimore chapter of the National Coalition of Black Lesbians and Gays was formed. A small Pride rally was held at Charles Center downtown.

In 1979, the center's newsletter became the first local gay newspaper, the *Baltimore Gay Paper;* the addition of paid advertising helped the center raise money. The paper and the switchboard operated out of board member Gail Vivino's basement at Twenty-eighth and Calvert Streets. A lesbian and gay rights bill was introduced to the Baltimore City Council. Pride became a block party held in front of the 31st Street Bookstore in Waverly. The first ever March on Washington for LGBT Rights was held in October 1979. In 1980, the center's president, Harvey Schwartz, raised $20,000 from businesses and individuals in less than six weeks for a down payment so the center could purchase a building at 241 West Chase Street. The city council voted down the gay rights bill after Archbishop Borders publicly opposed it. Pride became a festival in 1980, held downtown at Charles Plaza.

The 1980s saw a flowering of LGBT culture: Brother Help Thyself flourished, two LGBT theater companies produced plays that reflected positive characters, Womonspace became a program at the center, and Black and White Men Together was formed in 1982. There were gay student clubs, lesbian rock bands, art exhibits, a Lesbian and Gay Democratic Club, and large formal fundraisers to raise renovation funds for the center. The first Pride parade was held. Transgendered leader Tammy Carnes Ball served on the board of GLCCB, Lambda Rising Books opened at the center, and there was another LGBT newspaper (the *Baltimore Alternative*) as well as a lesbian newsletter (the *Women's Express*). Then came the second defeat of the gay rights bill by the vote in the Baltimore City Council in 1985.

The AIDS epidemic was the source of the second big transformation of the community. Health Education Resource Organization (HERO), begun by Dr. Bernie Branson, became Baltimore's first AIDS service provider in 1983. Local LGBT activists such as Scott Stamford, Dr. Sam Westrick, and Joyce Dennison responded to the crisis. By the end of the decade, there were over a dozen local AIDS organizations and city and state agencies devoted to dealing with HIV. In 1987, Lynda Dee and other organizers founded AIDS Action Baltimore for people with AIDS. The second National March on Washington was also held in 1987, and inspired local activists anew. Moveable Feast began delivering meals to people with AIDS. LGBT leader Liza Solomon became head of the State of Maryland's AIDS Administration.

The Baltimore Justice Campaign mobilized the community to pass the civil rights bill, finally, in 1988, with the support of Mayor Kurt Schmoke and council president Mary Pat Clarke. In 1988, the NAMES Project Memorial Quilt went on display at the Baltimore Museum of Art, commemorating those who had perished. Pride Day moved to Wyman Park Dell. The AIDS Walk was a huge success for HERO and other AIDS service providers. In 1989, the Chase Brexton Clinic became independent of the center, and the first Mayoral Task Force on Gay and Lesbian issues was appointed by Kurt Schmoke. In 1990, ACT UP Baltimore was founded by John Stuban. Churches and synagogues began to welcome LGBT people. In 1991, the first African American LGBT festival was held in St. Mary's Park. The Baltimore Justice Campaign became the Free State Justice Campaign (later Equality Maryland). Mayor Schmoke extended domestic partnership benefits to city employees in 1993, and Governor Schaefer issued an executive order barring discrimination against LGBT state employees that same year. Pride moved from Wyman Park Dell, to Towson State University, then back to the Dell, then to Druid Hill Park.

Johns Hopkins' SHARE AIDS research study continued, and lesbian leader Liza Solomon and the staff of the State AIDS Administration continued to provide AIDS education and funds for service providers to everyone.

OUTLoud, another local gay paper, began publishing in 2003. Transgender support groups began at the GLCCB and elsewhere, lobbied successfully for civil rights protection at the city and state level, and continue to progress.

Domestic partners found they could not get health benefits or pensions, or visit lovers admitted to ICUs. Lesbians, gay men, and transgendered people coming out of heterosexual unions had always had children, but now LGBT families began choosing to have children by adoption, alternative insemination, and foster care. The third wave of change crested as couples realized they could lose their children because a spouse had no legal standing. Then marriage equality became law in 2012, decades after Maryland became the first state in the union in 1973 to limit marriage to a man and a woman.

On January 1, 2013, Mayor Stephanie Rawlings-Blake presided over the first same-sex marriages in Maryland's history at a midnight ceremony at Baltimore City Hall.

PFLAG grew, and so did the Chase Brexton Clinic. The clinic moved as it grew to serve more clients with AIDS, and finally bought the Monumental Life Building on Charles Street in 2013. Metropolitan Community Church shared rented space in different churches, finally settling in its own space in 1998 with Rev. David Smith, in the sanctuary where Rev. Victoria Burson leads the congregation today.

The GLCCB moved to the Waxter Center in 2014. The new quarters did not include enough room for 40 years of history, so the University of Baltimore agreed to house the archival collection (used as one source of images for this book) in the basement of the Langsdale Library.

This book is not and cannot be the entire story of LGBT liberation in Baltimore. There is always more to a story. But it is a source, to record some of what happened, who was there, and where it all began in Baltimore. We said we were going to be the change we wanted to see, and we did it with style.

One

WHEN LGBT LIBERATION WAS NEW

Cheryl Parham, Baltimore activist, is in uniform at her Marine Corps anniversary in November 1973. Cheryl was a leader and served her community and city for years, proving she was, indeed, *Semper fidelis*. (Courtesy Cheryl Parham.)

John Waters, a twisted genius, filmmaker, witty writer, and visionary, is perhaps the most famous gay man in Baltimore. If not, he has certainly done his best to be unforgettable. His filmmaking career began in 1964, and includes *Pink Flamingos, Desperate Living, Serial Mom, Pecker*, and, of course, *Hairspray*. All these films are set in Baltimore. (Courtesy GLCCB Archives and John Waters.)

The women of the lesbian feminist Ida Brayman Collective of the early 1970s lived in this house at 950 Homestead Street in Waverly. (Courtesy Jim White.)

The Metropolitan Community Church was located at 2233 St. Paul Street from 1976 until 1978. The building had previously served as a manufacturing site for artificial limbs. In 1978, the building also served as the first home of a gay men's health clinic. The clinic then became a part of the Gay Community Center of Baltimore from 1978 until 1989, and in 1989 became the independent Chase Brexton Health Services. (Courtesy Jim White.)

This is the 1977 marriage photograph of Baltimorean Lisa Siegel (left) and Washingtonian Lou Parker Kelley. Marriage between two women in Maryland would not be legal until more than 30 years after this picture was made. (Author.)

Iconic lesbian writer Gertrude Stein lived here at 212 East Biddle Street from 1897 until 1900 with her brother Leo while she was in medical school at John Hopkins. She experienced her first romantic relationship with another woman during her time in Baltimore. In late 1899 or early 1900, she became enmeshed in a tortured love triangle, falling in love with a Bryn Mawr College graduate, May Bookstaver, who was romantically involved with one of Gertrude's fellow medical students, Mabel Haynes. (Courtesy Jim White.)

Diana Press was a small early lesbian feminist publishing house at 12 West Twenty-fifth Street. It was founded in 1972 during a time when few LGBT authors were being published by mainstream publishers, and it gave voice to lesbian authors who might not otherwise have been published. The press was housed in a basement office at this location from 1974 to 1977. Six row houses were razed in 2000 to make way for the CVS store that now stands at that site. (Courtesy Jim White.)

Leon's is the oldest continuously operating gay bar in Baltimore; it has been a gay bar since 1957. The building has housed bars with various names since the 1890s; it is called Leon's because its owner in the 1930s was Leon Lampe. Leon's is located at 870 Park Avenue in Mount Vernon. (Courtesy Jim White.)

The home of Dana Rethmeyer was located 928 North Charles Street, the location of some of the earliest meetings of the Baltimore Gay Alliance. BGA was the parent of the GLCCB. (Courtesy Jim White.)

The 31st Street Bookstore, a women's bookstore with a strong lesbian feminist presence, was established at 425 East Thirty-first Street in 1973 and closed in 1995. It served as a focal point in the lesbian feminist community. The bookstore sold the writings of lesbian and feminist authors, held readings and other events, and served as a hub for the women's community. Since 1995, the site of the 31st Street Bookstore has been occupied by Normal's Bookstore. (Courtesy Jim White.)

The sign for the 31st Street Bookstore is currently the largest artifact stored in the Special Collections GLCCB Archives at the University of Baltimore.

The Women's Liberation Center was located at 101 East Twenty-fifth Street; it provided space for the Lesbian Community Center from its founding in 1974 until its move to 3028 Greenmount Avenue in 1978. Many small nonprofit organizations had their offices on Twenty-fifth Street during this time, leading to the nickname for the stretch of Twenty-fifth Street between Howard Street and Greenmount Avenue as "Nonprofit Row." (Courtesy Jim White.)

Squeeze Louise, a lesbian band, is seen performing in the community space at the GLCCB in 1983.

The Bread and Roses Coffeehouse, housed at 424 East Thirty-first Street, was an outgrowth of the counterculture of the late 1960s and early 1970s. The Muses Collective, a lesbian production company, held many of its events here and at nearby Waverly Presbyterian Church and St. John's United Methodist Church. Artists such as Suede; Sanders, Kass & White; and Kate Clinton performed here. (Courtesy Jim White.)

The Lesbian Community Center was founded in 1974. It was located at 3028 Greenmount Avenue from 1978 until the early 1980s on the second floor of the People's Community Health Centers along with the offices of *Women: a Journal of Liberation*, an early and long-running national publication of the feminist movement with a strong lesbian presence. *Women: a Journal of Liberation* was established in 1969 and remained in publication until 1983. (Courtesy Jim White.)

Supporters of pro-gay mayoral candidate Billy Murphy at the Pride festival in 1983 include Kenn Hill (left) and Louis Hughes (right). (Courtesy Mardie Walker.)

Pictured on the left is Billy Murphy, a pro-gay mayoral candidate who ran against longtime mayor William Donald Schaefer in 1983. Murphy is waiting to address the crowd during that year's Pride festival. Beside Murphy, addressing the crowd, is gay activist and attorney Lee David Hoshall.

Beulah Lamont was a drag pageant coordinator for the Hippo and for Pride Day. This entrepreneur founded her own drag production company.

Baltimore's Washington Monument was the site of the first Pride rally in 1975. In 1984, a crowd of gay rights supporters, many wearing masks, gathered here in support of Baltimore City Council Bill 187, the gay rights bill. The demonstrators marched to the Inner Harbor, where they held a candlelight vigil in front of the Maryland Science Center. (Courtesy Jim White.)

Soon after its founding in 1975, the Baltimore Gay Alliance had its first rental quarters at 416 East 31 Street. Although tiny, the BGA's office was a sign of the growth of the group. (Courtesy Jim White.)

Lesbian bar Sherry's was located on Broadway in Upper Fells Point. The front was a straight bar; the back room was lesbian space.

The Club Hippo on Eager Street opened in 1972 and is famous for shows, dances, and good bartenders. Owner Chuck Bowers has been generously supporting Pride Day for years. After a 43-year run, the Hippo will close in late 2015. (Courtesy Jim White.)

Lesbian activist Gail Vivino was a John Hopkins medical school dropout who was employed by the Baltimore City Community Relations Commission. In 1977, she opened the basement of her home at 2745 North Calvert Street to GCCB's information and referral switchboard and a newspaper, the *Gay Paper*, operated by the center. The switchboard and the newspaper remained there until the center purchased a building at 241 West Chase Street in 1980. (Courtesy Jim White.)

Chris Mason (1949–1999) was a performer, LGBT activist, and wigmaker extraordinaire for John Waters's films as a member of the Dreamland crew. Chris supplied costumes (and, naturally, wigs) for the Camp of Music production at the Hippo. She also founded the satiric Order of St. Dymphna (patron saint of the insane) for zany women everywhere. (Courtesy John Waters)

Harvey Schwartz was a past GLCCB president and was the leader who raised the money for the down payment for the building on Chase Street in less than six weeks. He was also the first paid executive director of GLCCB and the first paid ad rep for the *Gay Paper*.

The health clinic, counseling services, youth group, and meeting space for the Gay Community Center of Baltimore were located in basement quarters here at 2133 Maryland Avenue from 1978 until 1980. During that time, an information and referral switchboard and *Gay Paper*, which was published by the GCCB, were located in the basement of Gail Vivino's home at 2745 North Calvert Street. In 1980, all of the components of the GCCB were eventually unified in one location when a building was purchased at 241 West Chase Street. (Courtesy Jim White.)

Pictured at GLCCB in 1980 are, from left to right, leaders Mike Berlin, the center's attorney and Wolfe Foundation trustee; Rudi Forti, then director of the center's clinic (now the Chase Brexton Clinic); Paulette Young, the center's first president, Theatre Closet founder, star of Jane Chambers's *A Late Snow*, director of TC's production of Martin Sherman's *Bent*, Pride MC, and Gay Youth group facilitator; Jim Becker, BGA member, clinic, *Gay Paper*, and switchboard founder, GLCCB's bylaws expert, AIDS activist, and OUTloud founder and publisher; and the author, who was *Gay Paper* founder, Theatre Closet and Venus Rising Theater founder and playwright, Baltimore Justice Campaign leader, and Pride Day chair.

These are the front doors of the GLCCB at 241 West Chase Street, Baltimore. (Courtesy Jim White.)

The 1981 Pride Festival was held at Charles Plaza in downtown Baltimore. Here, the women's rock band Lucretia is performing.

John Hopkins University's News-Letter Office was the original home of the Gay Student Alliance of JHU in the 1970s. (Courtesy Jim White.)

Vince Gomes of Dignity, a group for LGBT Catholics, is shown here. The Baltimore chapter of Dignity formed in 1973; it was one of the earliest LGBT religious organizations in Baltimore. Gomes was one of its first members.

Dane Rethmeyer of the Baltimore Gay Alliance waves the Maryland flag at the Stonewall riots' 25th anniversary in New York in 1994.

St. John's United Methodist Church at 2640 St. Paul Street served as the home for the Metropolitan Community Church (MCC) on three separate occasions. Baltimore MCC was founded in 1972, and it had been in a total of 11 locations prior to the congregation's purchase of its current location at 405 West Monument Street in 1998. St. John's served as MCC's home from 1972 until 1974, 1980 until 1981, and 1985 until 1989. St. John's also provided space for women's music concerts and other LGBT community events. (Courtesy Jim White.)

Anti-gay protestors are shown in front of Baltimore's City Hall in 1980. LGBT activists and supporters mounted three attempts to pass a gay rights bill in Baltimore. The first failed attempt was in 1979–1980. The second failed attempt was in 1984–1985. The third attempt, this one successful, was in 1987–1988.

Two

OUT AND NEVER
GOING BACK

This is the Baltimore Lesbian and Gay Democratic Club's entry in the 1987 Pride Parade. Club members pictured are Steve Cody (left) and Richard Oloizia. (Courtesy Mardie Walker.)

Shown here is a view of the 1983 Pride Festival from the Chase Brexton Clinic's third-floor windows at the GLCCB. The 1980 and 1981 festivals were held in Charles Plaza. The 1982 festival was rained out. The first year that the event was held in front of the GLCCB was 1983. (Courtesy Chase Brexton Clinic.)

Lynn Cook and the Bad Girls are shown performing during GLCCB's 1985 Pride Festival on Chase Street.

Activists are picketing in front of Baltimore City Hall in 1985 to support the passage of City Council Bill 187, the lesbian and gay civil rights bill. The Baltimore City Council was reluctant to bring the bill out of committee for a floor vote.

David Carroll, GLCCB board member and past president, was the first openly gay man appointed to a governor's cabinet. He was secretary of the environment beginning in 1993, when William Donald Schaefer was governor.

Dignity Baltimore sponsored activist Ginny Apuzzo to speak in Baltimore in 1982. Pictured are, from left to right, the author, GLCCB vice president; Ellie Eines of the New Wave Singers and Chesapeake Squares; Mary Emery, GLCCB treasurer; Lynn Cook, Pride entertainer; and Sarah Cannon, GLCCB building chair and Womonspace founder.

Bryon Predika is pictured at the Baltimore Lesbian and Gay Democratic Club booth at Pride in 1987. His life partner, Jon DeHart, was the director of GLCCB for many years and handled Pride logistics. Bryon coordinated many Pride parades, including the first, in 1983, which was a mere three blocks long. (Courtesy Mardie Walker.)

Metropolitan Community Church choir performed at 1987 Pride Day, when it was held in the 200 block of West Chase Street in front of the GLCCB. Deborah McCallum is at the center, while Rev. Jennie Boyd Bull is on the right. (Courtesy Mardie Walker.)

At the Baltimore Lesbian and Gay Democratic Club booth at 1987 Pride are Mardie Walker (right) and Kurt Kugelberg. (Courtesy Mardie Walker.)

Dakota Scott-Hoffman was a Gay Youth member in 1979, GLCCB switchboard cochair, Black and White Men Together leader, caregiver for Arthur Stutsman and Harvey Lee Hoffman, and a SHARE employee in 1986. (Courtesy Dakota Scott-Hoffman.)

Mark Phillips is promoting the GLCCB's information and referral switchboard (and himself) in a Pride parade on Park Avenue in Mount Vernon in the mid-1980s. Mark was also a garden columnist for the *BGP*.

Baltimore Justice Campaign activists are seen in this April 1988 photograph, taken during a press conference held to promote the passage of City Council Bill 187, the lesbian and gay rights bill.

The lesbian and gay rights bill's supporters enjoy a victory party at BJC member Steve Glassman's Baltimore condo in June 1988. (Courtesy Mardie Walker.)

The Gay and Lesbian Switchboard banner is displayed on a car during a Pride parade.

Women of GLCCB's Womonspace enjoy a lighthearted moment in the fourth-floor meeting space at 241 West Chase in 1989.

The Woman's Growth Center, a feminist therapy collective with many lesbian therapists and clients, was established in 1973. WGC was located at 2641 North Charles Street from 1986 until 2000. Since that time, it has been located at 5209 York Road. Between 1980 and 1985, it was located at 339 East Twenty-fifth Street. From 1973 to 1979, it was at various locations. (Courtesy Jim White.)

Baltimore Justice Campaign activist Shannon Avery (left) listens to attorney Deborah McCallum address the crowd at a Baltimore City Hall rally in 1988 in support of the passage of the city's lesbian and gay rights bill. Avery is currently a Baltimore City circuit court judge.

AIDS Action Baltimore participates in the 2004 Pride Parade on Charles Street.

Scott Stamford (1948–1987) was one of the founders of HERO and a vocal, vivid, early AIDS activist.

HERO's banner is carried by volunteers in a parade near Druid Hill Park.

HERO, Baltimore's first AIDS service and education organization (founded in 1983), was located on the eighth floor of the Medical Arts Building at 101 West Read Street. The Chase Brexton Clinic was also located here from 1989 until 1994. (Courtesy Jim White.)

Joyce Kramer served as the volunteer coordinator for HERO and later as the organization's development director. She helped elect delegate Salima Siler Marriott, among others. This feminist was also a former Baltimore City schoolteacher, a community organizer, and a published author (*Invisible No More*, written with Renee Fisher and Jean Peelen).

Lesbian Marge Owens, pictured in the HERO office in 1984, was the longest-serving volunteer for the organization, working particularly with the buddy program. The buddy program provided care and support for people with AIDS and relied heavily on hundreds of volunteers.

Chris Camp, a HERO staff member, shows off the program for AIDS Walk 1988.

The Brother Help Thyself contingent is marching in a Pride parade. Brother Help Thyself is a longtime organization in Baltimore's gay male leather-aficionado community that provides grants for LGBT organizations through its fundraising efforts.

Longtime LGBT rights activist Ann Gordon is applauded at her rousing speech at the Baltimore Justice Campaign's victory party at Hippo when CC 187, the civil rights bill, passed the Baltimore City Council in May 1988. Later in 1988, Gordon was honored by the Maryland Women's Law Center as Woman of the Year. (Courtesy Ann Gordon.)

The Girls Just Want to Have Drums contingent marches in a Pride parade. (Courtesy Mardie Walker.)

When the health clinic of the GLCCB became independent of the center in 1989, it chose a name for the newly created organization from the names of the streets where the GLCCB was located from 1980 until 2014, at the intersection of Chase and Brexton Streets. (Courtesy Jim White.)

AIDS researcher Dr. B. Frank Polk of the Johns Hopkins School of Public Health made a huge contribution to the lives of people living with AIDS prior to his death from brain cancer in 1988.

New Wave Singers perform at 1987 Pride in the 200 block of West Chase Street in front of the GLCCB. (Courtesy Mardie Walker.)

The cast and crew of Jane Chambers's lesbian comedy, *My Blue Heaven*, performed at the GLCCB in 1985, show what a kick they get out of theater. Producer (and this book's author) Louise Parker Kelley is pictured on the far right in a red-striped dress. (Author.)

Three unidentified men use their couch for the most comfortable viewing location on the parade route during a Pride parade on Maryland Avenue.

A 1989 "Stop the Silence" magnet, advertising the anti-LGBT violence project hotline of the BJC and the GLCCB Switchboard, is show here. (Author.)

Kathy Chavis was GLCCB's executive director from 1988 to 1989. (Courtesy Dakota Scott-Hoffman.)

The Torch was a gay bar located at 411 East Thirty-second Street from 1983 until 1986. In 1984, Henry Westray, along with other men active in Black and White Men Together, an interracial group for gay men, sued the owner of the Torch for racial discrimination because of the carding practices used at the entrance to the bar. Henry and the other plaintiffs from Black and White Men Together won the suit. (Courtesy Jim White.)

A memorial quilt panel for Teddy, a gay Baltimorean who died of AIDS, appears as part of the NAMES Project at the 1987 display. (Author.)

The Candlelight Vigil for People with AIDS was held in conjunction with the display of the NAMES Project at the Baltimore Museum of Art in June 1988.

A fundraiser for mayoral candidate Kurt Schmoke is pictured at the B&O Railroad Museum in 1987. Schmoke is in the red suspenders. Sen. Barbara Mikulski is to the right of the speaker.

The dell of Wyman Park served as the home for Baltimore's annual LGBT pride festivals from 1988 until 1996. From 1983 until 1987, the festival was held in the 200 block of West Chase Street where the GLCCB was located. Growth of the event led to its relocation to Wyman Park. Further growth and drainage problems in the dell prompted another relocation, to Druid Hill Park in 1997.

A mermaid with lobster and whale participates in a Pride parade on Maryland Avenue, just below North Avenue. The Pride festival was held in Wyman Park from 1988 until 1996. During those years, the parade was held on Maryland Avenue. The parade began at the Gallery Bar and ran north to the park.

A contingent from the Gay and Lesbian Switchboard, a program of the GLCCB, is shown at a Pride parade on Maryland Avenue.

Chase Sutherland, the first manager of Lambda Rising, is pictured in front of the bookstore. Lambda Rising, an LGBT bookstore, was located on the first floor of the GLCCB from 1986 until 2008.

The Baltimore Men's Chorus performs at the 1987 Pride Day.

Since so much of Baltimore's visible lesbian feminist community was focused in the Charles Village and Waverly neighborhoods, Abell Avenue was nicknamed "Lesbian Lane" because of the large number of lesbian-identified women who lived on those blocks during the early days of the LGBT movement. The rainbow-hued homes there are among the most colorful in Charles Village. (Courtesy Jim White.)

Portions of the Names Project Quilt were on display at the Baltimore Museum of Art during the 1988 Pride Festival, which was held in the dell of Wyman Park adjacent to the Baltimore Museum of Art. This was the first time the quilt was shown at a museum. (Courtesy Laura Steber and the *Baltimore Gay Paper*.)

Playwright Martin Sherman, pictured here, was the author of *Bent*, a play about the gay men persecuted by the Nazis and forced to wear pink triangles in the extermination camps. Theatre Closet's Baltimore production in the 1980s, directed by Paulette Young and featuring Allen Beall, helped popularize the use of the inverted pink triangle as a symbol of pride and survival. (Author.)

The cast of *Collective Consciousness*, an ensemble comedy by local lesbian playwright and author of this book Louise Parker Kelley, is shown in performance at the GLCCB in 1982. Note that the backdrop, designed by director Pat Cote, features political buttons popular at the time.

An award was presented to the author in 1983 by the GLCCB president and executive director. This illuminated certificate was designed and illustrated by Bill Newhall and features the seal of the center. (Author.)

GLCCB's Brager Award was given annually to outstanding volunteers in honor of their work and in memory of a mensch, Elliott Brager. This one was awarded to Richard Oloizia, who served as chair of the Switchboard for over a decade. (Author.)

Located in a basement office at 36 West Twenty-fifth Street from 1991 until it ceased publication in 2000, the *Baltimore Alternative* was founded in 1986 by Bill Urban, a former ad salesman for the *Baltimore Gay Paper*. The *Baltimore Alternative* was especially strong on coverage of the early days of the AIDS epidemic in Baltimore, and its success proved that Baltimore was big enough to support two LGBT newspapers. (Courtesy Jim White.)

This highway sign was the first to include the LGBT community as part of the Adopt-a-Highway Litter Control program run by the State Highway Administration. Pictured are some of those who were taking a stand as Lesbians for Change.

This St. Dymphna medal was presented by Chris Mason to the author in 1993 after her work on Riley's *The Camp of Music* at the Hippo. (Author.)

In this publicity shot for AIDS Walk 1990 are GLCCB and HERO fundraiser and activist Steve Schavitz, left; Frances Draper of the Baltimore Afro American newspaper, center; and Andy Barasda of HERO, right.

Three

FROM STRENGTH
TO STRENGTH

The 1991 Pride planning committee is assembled for a picture. Mardie Walker, president of the GLCCB, is in the center of the photograph wearing glasses and an orange shirt. (Courtesy Mardie Walker.)

Members of the Man Alive contingent (a methadone program for recovering addicts) are shown walking together at AIDS Walk in 1992.

ACT UP (AIDS Coalition to Unleash Power) and the People With Aids Coalition are pictured during a Pride parade on Maryland Avenue. Pictured on the left in the foreground is John Stuban, who founded the Baltimore chapter of ACT UP in 1990.

The Baltimore Justice Campaign and the GLCCB sponsored this billboard to enhance LGBT awareness in 1992. (Photograph by Tim Ford, courtesy Louis Hughes Jr.)

The opening scene from *The Camp of Music*, written by Joanne Riley, was performed at the Hippo in 1993. (Author.)

PFLAG (Parents, Families and Friends of Lesbians and Gays) marches during a Pride parade.

Gay + Lesbian Families + Friends march during AIDS Walk. Bebe Verdery (left) was one of the founding members of the group as well as of the Baltimore Justice Campaign.

A contingent from the People With Aids Coalition marches during a Pride parade. The PWA Coalition was an advocacy and support group active during the height of the AIDS epidemic.

Ed Sherman staffs the then-named GCCB booth at the Baltimore City Fair in 1978. Note the Parents of Gays poster and the repetition of the word *gay*.

SAIM (Sufficient As I Am), the GLCCB youth group, and Womonspace, another program of the community center, are both seen marching in a Pride parade. The University of Baltimore, now the home of the GLCCB Archives, is in the background.

The SAIM LGBT youth group of GLCCB prepares to leave on a bus trip to New York City in December 2000. The members are posing in front of the center on Chase Street. (Courtesy Louis Hughes.)

Janet Goldstein (left) and Shirley Hartwell, employees of the 31st Street Bookstore, pose together in the store in 1989. (Photograph by Phyllis A. Mobley, courtesy of Janet Goldstein and Theresa Palomar.)

The 31st Street Bookstore Cooperative contingent is seen marching in the Washington, DC, Pride parade.

Cindy Schwartz (left) and Laura
Neuman (right) are at the
NOW table at Pride in Druid
Hill Park in the 1990s.

Jane Troxell was the manager of
Lammas Baltimore. The 31st Street
Bookstore was sold to Lammas in
1995, moved to Cathedral Street
in the same building as the Chase
Brexton Clinic, and closed in 1996.

Rev. David Smith of MCC Baltimore gives two thumbs-up to MCC's then new sanctuary at 405 West Monument Street in Baltimore.

Local lesbian leaders and their allies are shown in international costumes during a Baltimore parade in 1990.

The late, great Elliott Brager (far right, with microphone), GLCCB's premier fundraiser, is with president Mardie Walker, on his left, and board members Glenda Rider and Joaquin Alvarez in 1990 at one of Brager's many successful formal fundraisers.

Partygoers at an AIDS fundraiser (for HERO Lifesongs 1991) include, from left to right, host Alexander Baer, hospitality chair Bonnie Dubin, Mark Dubin, Louise Goodman, and Mitzi Glick.

In 1999, the participants in the Swim for Life AIDS fundraiser gather prior to diving into the Chesapeake Bay.

Greg Satorie, pictured in the foreground at the right, is seen during a Pride parade on Charles Street.

Advocates of the passage of domestic partnership legislation picket at the University of Maryland at Baltimore in downtown Baltimore. Activists lobbied for domestic partnership after the US Congress passed DOMA and marriage equality seemed impossible.

Maryland's Free State Justice Campaign contingent marches in a Pride parade. Free State Justice was Maryland's first statewide LGBT political advocacy organization. It is known today as Equality Maryland.

New Year's Eve revelers are at the Port in a Storm, a longtime lesbian bar, in 2000.

The Lesbian Avengers are pictured "coming out of the closet" during a street theater–style demonstration in front of Baltimore's World Trade Center at the Inner Harbor. The Baltimore chapter of the Avengers was formed in 1995.

Baltimore activists are shown at the third national March for LGBT Rights in Washington, DC, in 1993.

This is a team from Womonspace, a program for women at the GLCCB, at the pro-abortion March for Women's Lives in Washington, DC, in 1989.

The women of FIST (Females Investigating Sexual Terrain) appear at the Baltimore-Washington Convention in 1991. Pictured on the far left is former GLCCB treasurer Glenda Rider.

The GLCCB contingent is marching in a Pride parade on Charles Street. The University of Baltimore is in the background.

Greg Satorie, Mr. Maryland Leather 1996, is seen in the 1996 Pride Parade.

This is the sign for the store the Leather Underground in Baltimore. (Photograph by Sarah Humble.)

Latina lesbians Dena (left) and Kay enjoy themselves at University of Maryland, Baltimore County's LGBT Prom Night in 1993.

Drag queen Bang Bang Ladash appears as the fabulous Divine in a Baltimore gay club. The original Divine (1945–1988) was a Baltimore icon, an actor first filmed by John Waters, and a Dreamland member emeritus.

Four

GAILY FORWARD

Gov. Parris Glendening, center, is pictured at the signing of the lesbian and gay rights bill in Annapolis in 2001.

GLCCB volunteers are marching during a Martin Luther King Day Parade in Baltimore in the first decade of the 21st century. Organizer of Black Pride and AIDS activist Carlton Smith is second from left, waving. (Courtesy Kevin Brown.)

Baltimore's gay newspaper, *OUTloud*, is well represented in a recent Pride parade. Pictured fifth from the left, with the mustache, is Steve Charing, a longtime LGBT community activist, journalist, and historian. (Courtesy *OUTloud* and Steve Charing.)

The office at 3200 Barclay Street is Baltimore City's 43rd State Legislative District Office for delegates Maggie McIntosh, Mary Washington, and Curt Anderson. McIntosh, who has served in the Maryland House of Delegates since 1992, was the first openly lesbian member of the General Assembly. She came out in 2001. Delegate Washington, who has served since 2011, is the first openly lesbian African American member of the General Assembly. Both were active in the efforts to pass the same sex marriage bill in 2012. (Courtesy Jim White.)

Donna Cartwright is a retired copresident of the American Federation of Labor–Congress of Industrial Organization's Pride at Work, the LGBT constituency group of the labor movement, and continues to serve as a board member. She was also a founding board member of the National Center for Transgender Equality, is a Baltimore resident, and has been active in transgender support and advocacy groups both locally and nationally. (Courtesy Donna Cartwright.)

To be young, gifted, gay, and black at Morgan State University works for these student leaders. Pictured are, from left to right, Shaleque Hinton, Khari Malik, and Coronado "CJ" Dyer at a campus planning meeting for the Peer Educators of SEX ME (Safe Experiences Xcite Me) in 2015. SEX ME is a safe sex program funded by the Maryland Department of Health and Mental Hygiene's AIDS Administration. (Author.)

Mayor Stephanie Rawlings-Blake, on the left, stands with her staff member Jim Scales (center) and his husband, Bill Tasker, on their wedding night. The mayor married the two men just after midnight on January 1, 2013, making the couple the first to marry legally in Maryland—and the mayor of Baltimore the first to officiate at a same-sex marriage in the state. (Courtesy Steve Charing.)

Rik Newton-Treadway is pictured in his snazzy red leather jacket. Rik, a leader in the GLCCB's Gay Youth group in the 1970s and 1980s, helps produce drag entertainment at Pride Day and continuously raises money for charity via the leather community events along with his husband, Paulie Newton-Treadway. (Courtesy Rik Newton-Treadway.)

Baltimore County transgender rights activists and their allies were able to get civil rights protection passed in 2012. Pictured here are, from left to right, transgendered leaders Mara Drummond, Mark Patro, Dana Beyer, and Sharon Brackett. (Courtesy Dana Beyer.)

Shown here is 1111 North Charles Street, the gorgeous and expansive headquarters and Mount Vernon clinic location of Chase Brexton Health Care, which has several other locations. Chase Brexton continues to be proud of its LGBT roots. (Courtesy Jim White.)

Established in 1987, AIDS Action Baltimore is currently located here, at 11 East Eager Street. It is dedicated to the support and education of people with HIV and the prevention of HIV. (Courtesy Jim White.)

Gov. Martin O'Malley signs the Marriage Equality Bill in Annapolis in March 2012. In the picture are many activists, including delegates Maggie McIntosh and Mary Washington, both Baltimore lesbians, in the second row on the right. The referendum on the bill (Question 6) passed in November 2012 and became law on January 1, 2013. (Courtesy Equality Maryland.)

This lesbian couple was legally married at MCC Baltimore on June 7, 2014, by Pastor Burson (far left). Coraline F. Jones-Ramirez is at center, in a wedding veil, and Angela T. Jones-Ramirez is on the right. (Courtesy Angela T. Jones-Ramirez.)

The wedding ceremony of Coraline F. Jones-Ramirez and Angela T. Jones-Ramirez is blessed (and legal) in Charm City. (Courtesy Angela T. Jones-Ramirez)

John Palen (left), of SHARE, the Chase Brexton Clinic board, and the HRSA director, married John Hannay (right), of GLCCB, the Free State Justice Campaign, the chief of HIV Prevention Services, MD AIDS Administration, on August 24, 2013, at Baltimore's Memorial Episcopal Church. They were the first Maryland male couple granted a second-parent adoption (both adults became legal parents of an adopted child) in 1998. (Courtesy John Hannay.)

In August 2011, Twila McDonough, a retired Johns Hopkins Hospital nurse (left), and local attorney Ann Singleton were wed at the Supreme Court. They did so with a Washington, DC, marriage license, since it was not legal for two women to marry in Maryland at the time. Note the wedding ring on Twila's finger. The marriage was performed by Rev. Craig Sparks of Columbia United Christian Church of Maryland. (Courtesy Twila McDonough and Ann Singleton.)

Twila McDonough (left) and Ann Singleton pose on the courthouse steps on their wedding day. Along with LGBT people everywhere today, they look to the Supreme Court to protect their rights as a married couple. (Courtesy Twila McDonough and Ann Singleton.)

Rev. Victoria L. Burson is pictured in the pastor's study at Metropolitan Community Church of Baltimore in the summer of 2014. MCC Baltimore, which began in 1972, is the oldest continuously operating LGBT cultural and spiritual organization in the city. (Courtesy MCC Baltimore.)

This is a Jewish marriage contract (*ketubah*), written in Hebrew and English, between the author and Jessica Weissman, from May 19, 2013. The ketubah was designed by artist Betsy Tuetsch. (Author and Jessica Weissman.)

Jack Garman was the manager of Lambda Rising Baltimore at 241 West Chase Street and a Baltimore activist. He is in the store along with bookseller Debbie (behind the counter) as they prepare LR for an event in 1992.

This is HERO's AIDS Walk 1994 Steering Committee. Shown, from left to right, are Michael Snowden, Deborah McCallum, Charlie Brown, Ed Ladd (tall man in the back), John Gizinski, Jeff Walstrum, Sandra Skidmore, Tom Glaser, Bob Linden, and Howard Wrench. Graphic designer Jeff McIlhaney's notorious condom posters (once shredded by the state government and later reissued without Governor Schaefer's name on them) are displayed on the walls.

Owners Jac (left) and Walter of the Gallery Bar pose with the trophies awarded by GLCCB for their bar's Pride float.

The birthday party at the Drinkery on Read Street in 2014 for Doris Stuchinsky, longtime bartender at Leon's, featured this delighted DJ. (Courtesy the Drinkery.)

Staci Maxwell, former Miss Gay Maryland, won a look-alike contest as country singer and actress Reba McEntire. Later, she was denied the title, but McEntire herself supported her and invited Staci to be a special concert guest.

Drag queen Josie Foster performs in purple at Grand Central.

Scott Baum is pictured on the left, and Ron Crognale is on the right. Baum was a former editor of GLCCB's newspaper, which was renamed *Gay Life* in the late 1990s, and Crognale was its artistic director.

Anthony McCarthy was a former editor of *Gay Life*, then a newspaper, now a monthly magazine.

Jay Finlayson, GLCCB building chair, stands in the *Baltimore Gay Paper* (BGP) office at the GLCCB in 2000. (Courtesy Dakota Scott-Hoffman.)

Shawna Alexander, drag performer and producer, is shown at 2001 Pride Day in Druid Hill Park. She is Baltimore's Queen of Comedy and was named Activist of the Year in 2013.

Governor O'Malley signs the bill known variously as SB-212, the Gender Identity Anti-Discrimination Act, or the Fairness for All Marylanders Act, enacted to protect the civil rights of the transgender community in 2014. (Courtesy Dana Beyer.)

Lynda Dee of AIDS Action Baltimore (left), former Speaker of the House, award-winning native Baltimorean, and congressional leader Nancy Pelosi (center), and the author are seen at the GLCCB Hometown Heroes Brunch in October 2013. (Courtesy Jay W. Photos.)

GLCCB Archives committee volunteers Arnie VandeBrake and Patrick Alexander examine some of the documents they organized for transfer to the University of Baltimore Langsdale Library Special Collections Department in 2013. (Courtesy Dan McEvily and Patrick Alexander.)

DISCOVER THOUSANDS OF LOCAL HISTORY BOOKS FEATURING MILLIONS OF VINTAGE IMAGES

Arcadia Publishing, the leading local history publisher in the United States, is committed to making history accessible and meaningful through publishing books that celebrate and preserve the heritage of America's people and places.

Find more books like this at
www.arcadiapublishing.com

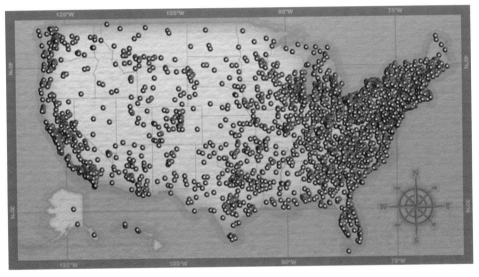

Search for your hometown history, your old stomping grounds, and even your favorite sports team.

Joel Tinsley-Harris is the current executive director of the GLCCB. He is pictured here in his office at the Waxter Center. (Courtesy Steve Charing.)

The Waxter Center, at 1000 Cathedral Street, is now the home of the GLCCB (on the third floor) as well as the hall for Chesapeake Squares dance group and many different Baltimore senior groups. (Courtesy Jim White.)